TEST COLOR PAGE

Thank you for choose this coloring book.
I hope you will have fun.

Merry *Christmas*

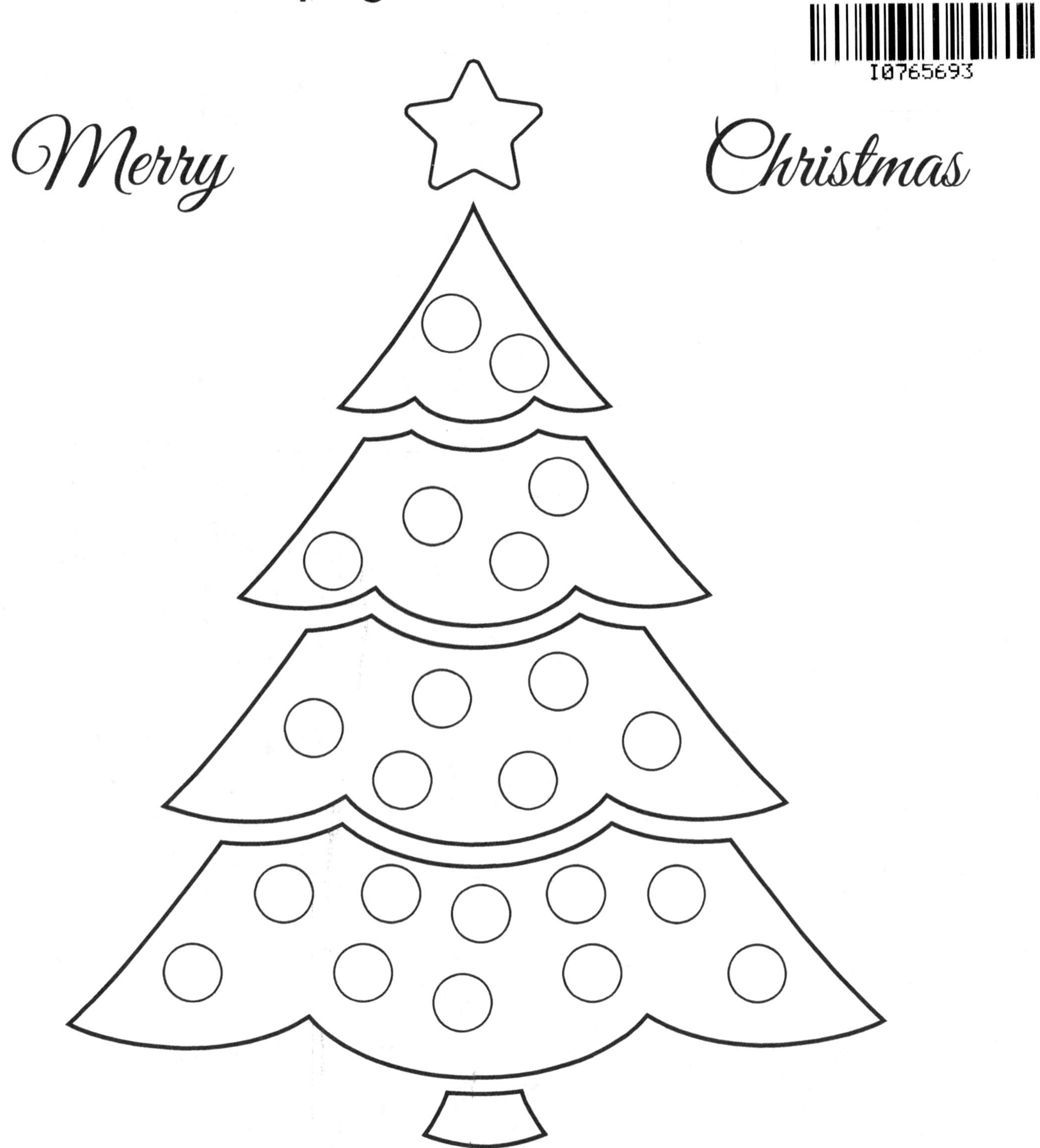

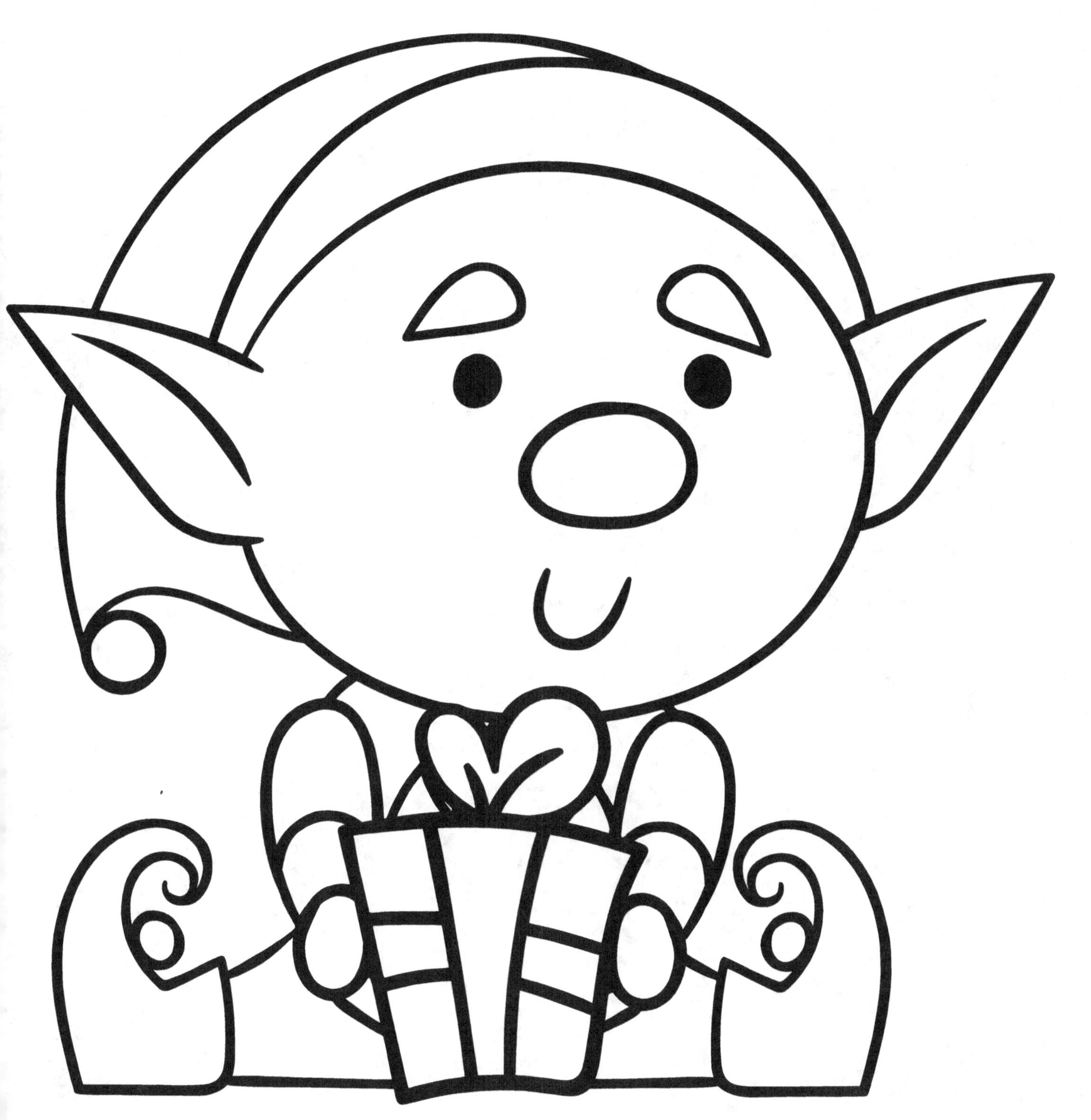

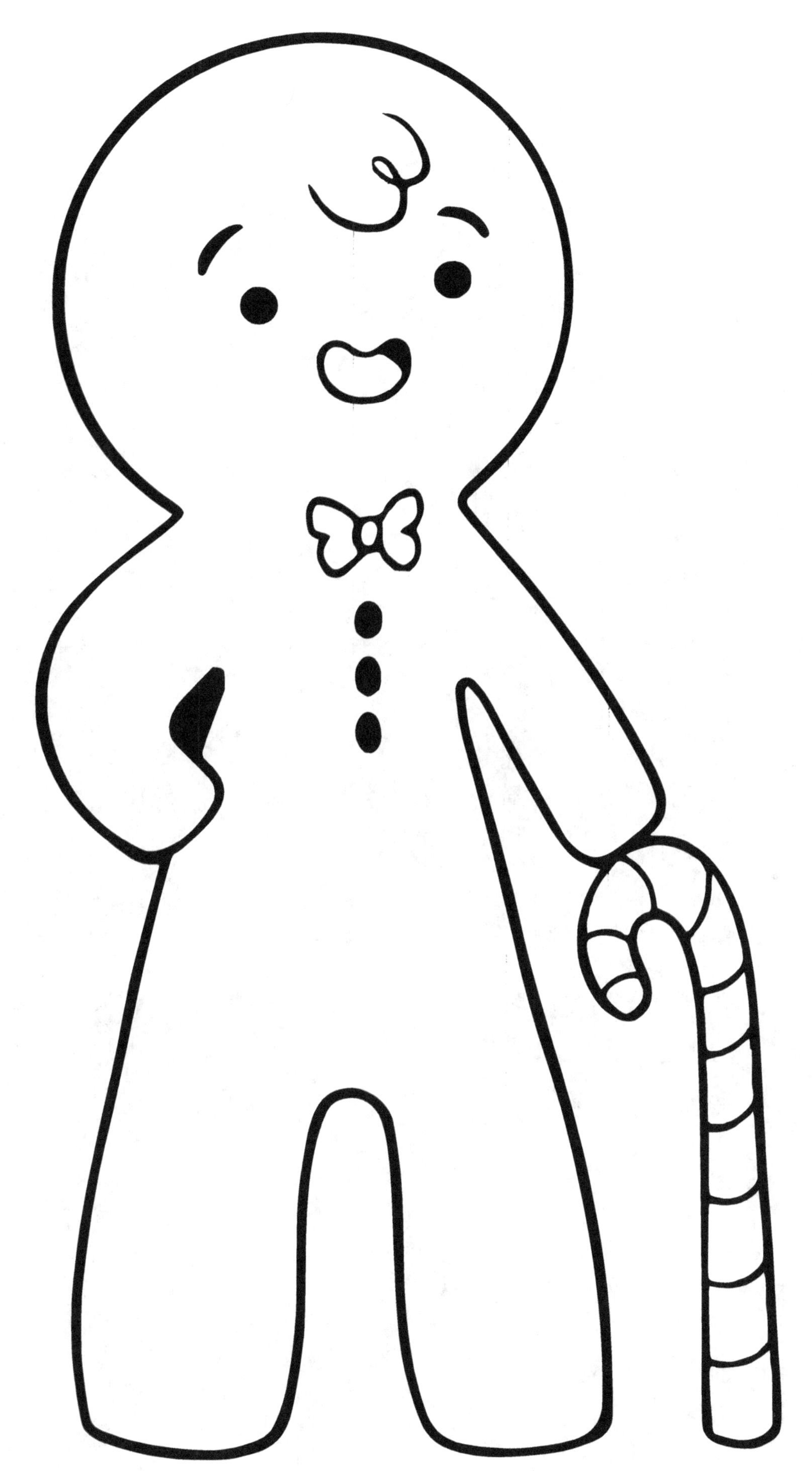

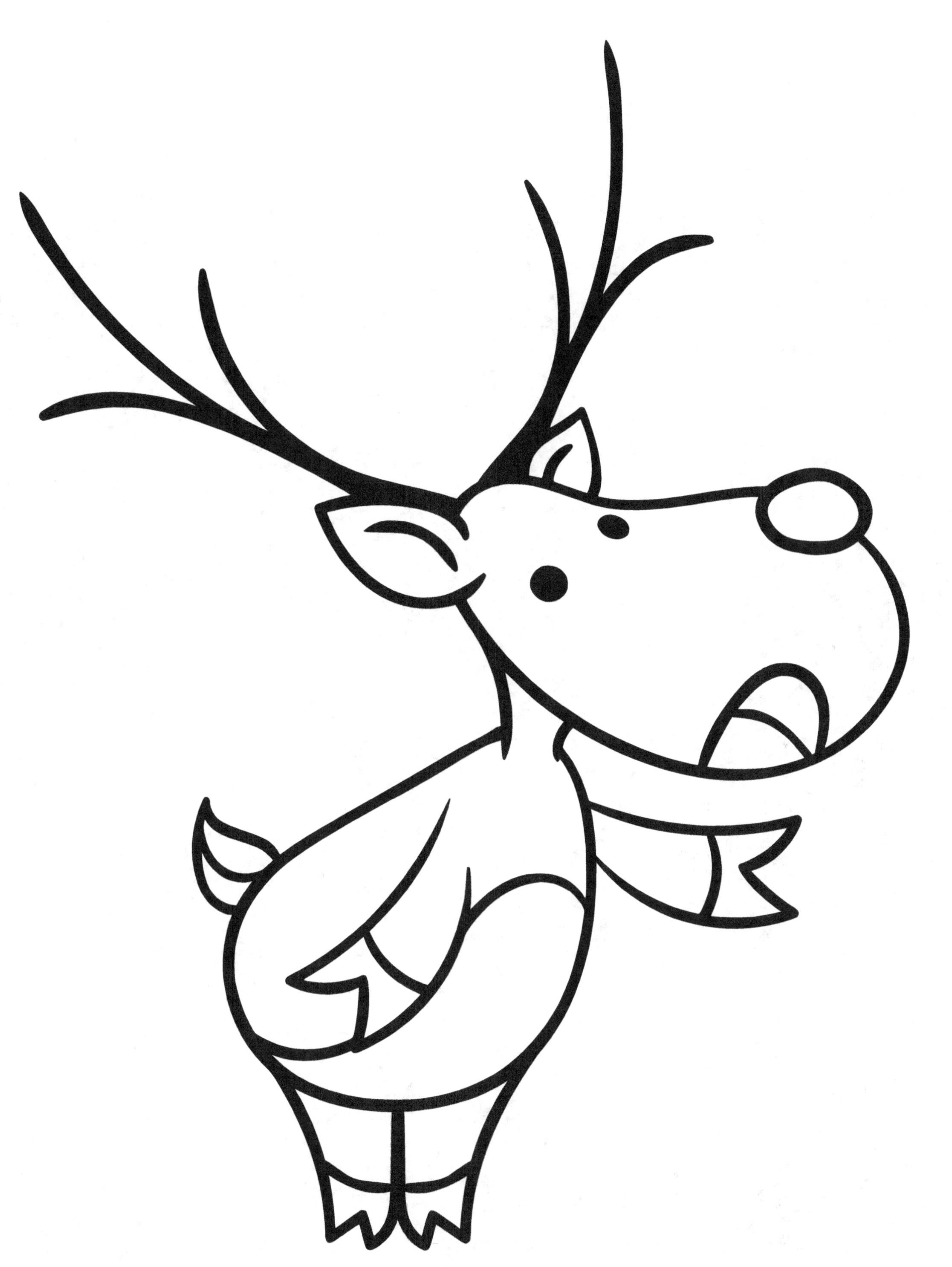

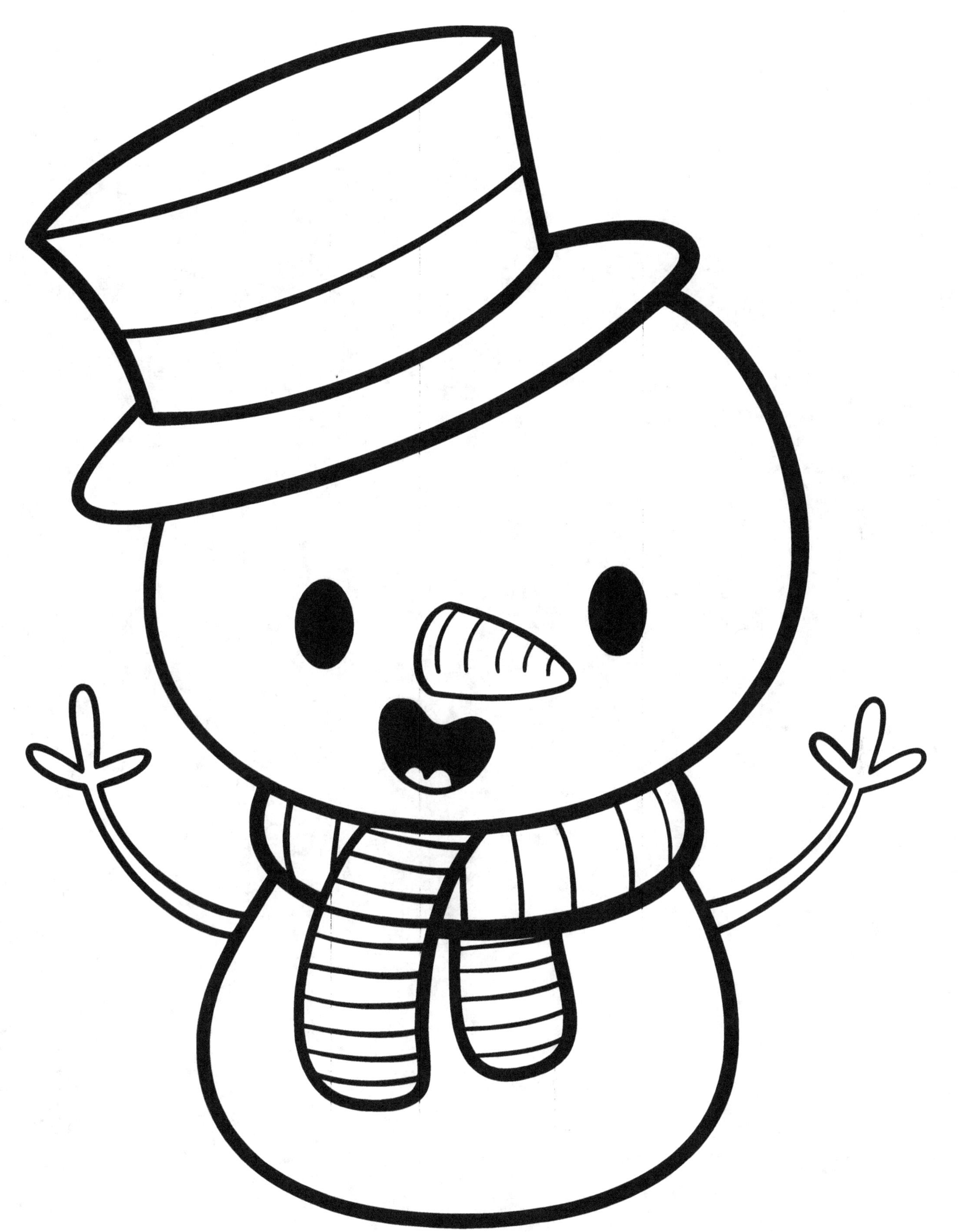

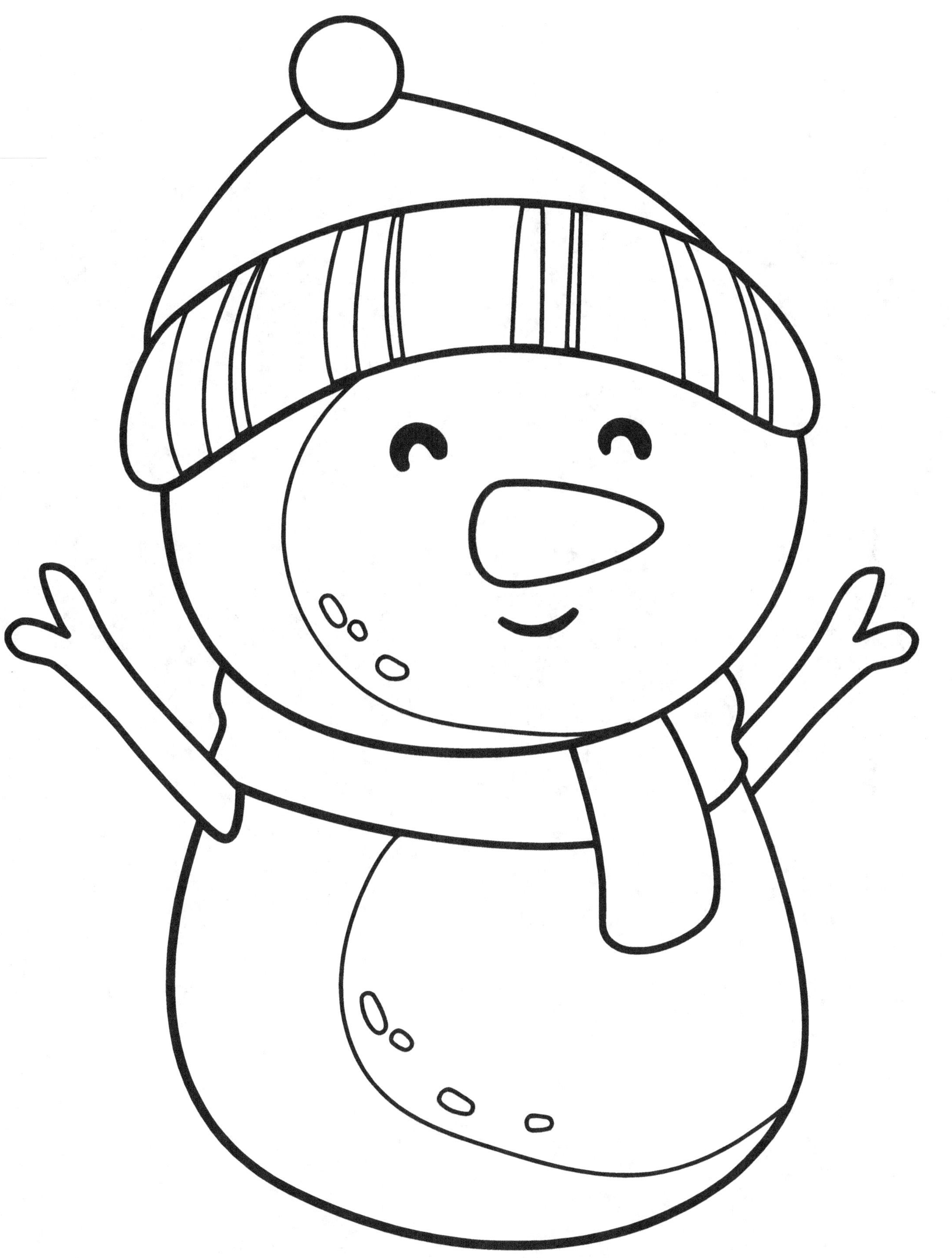

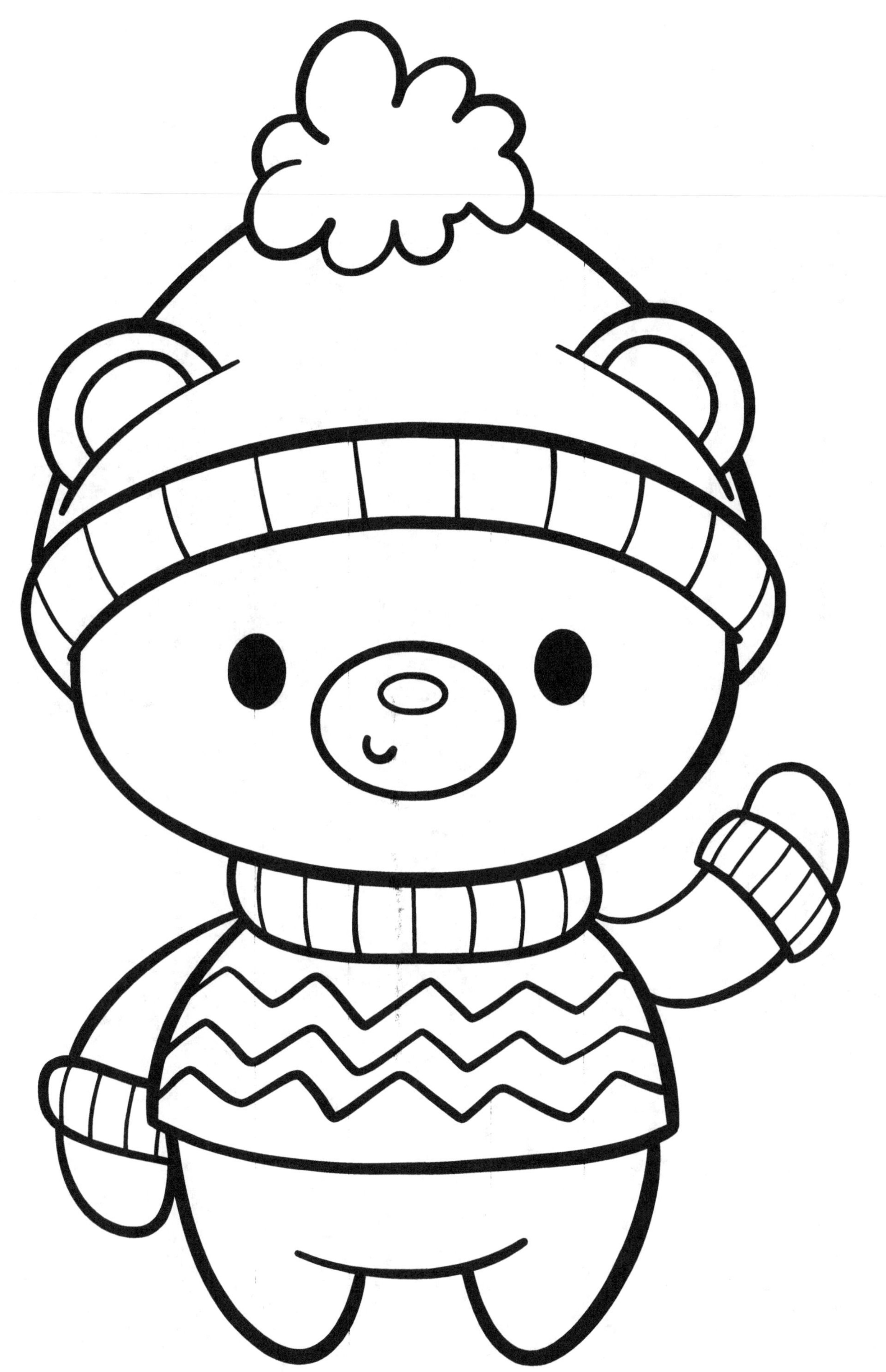

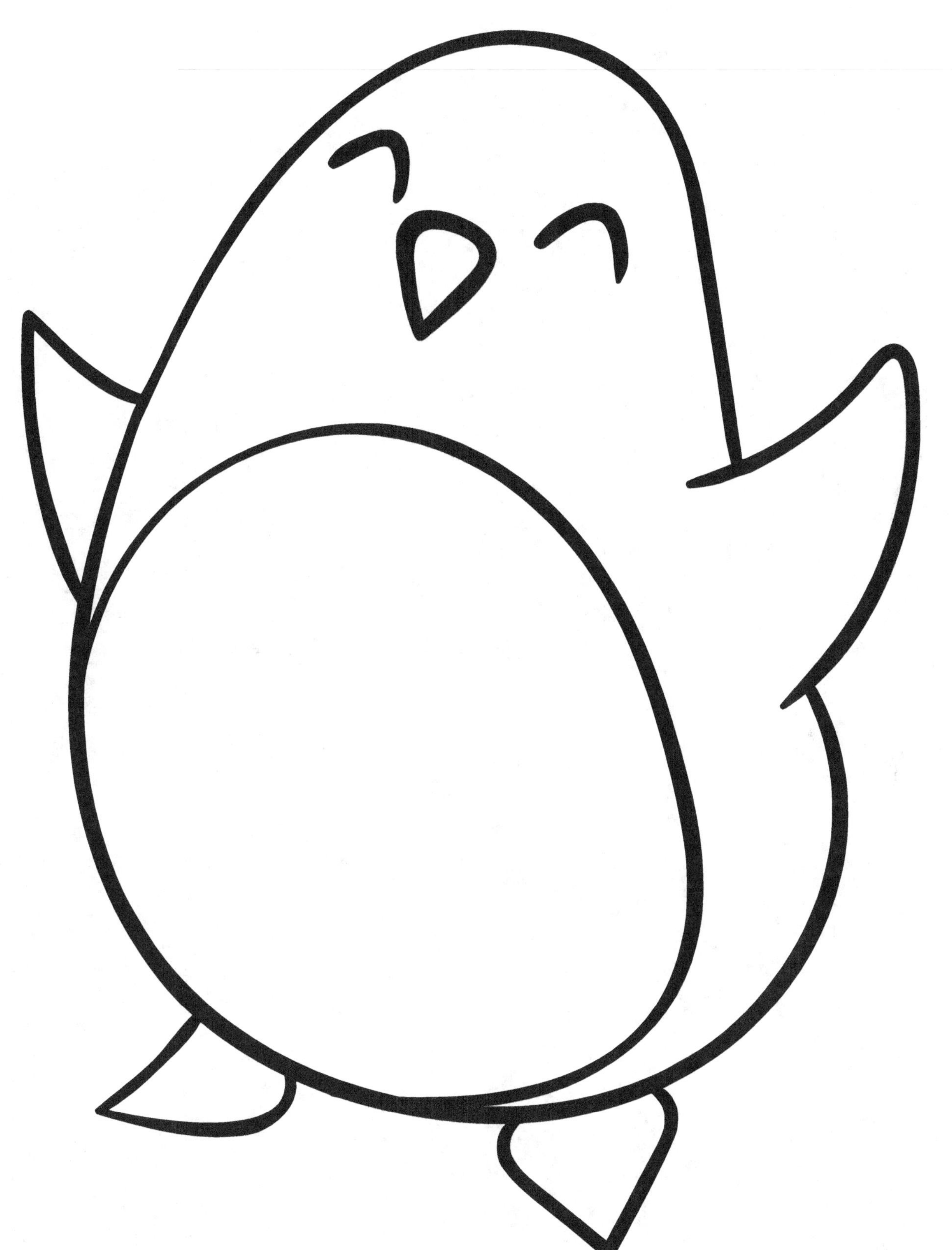

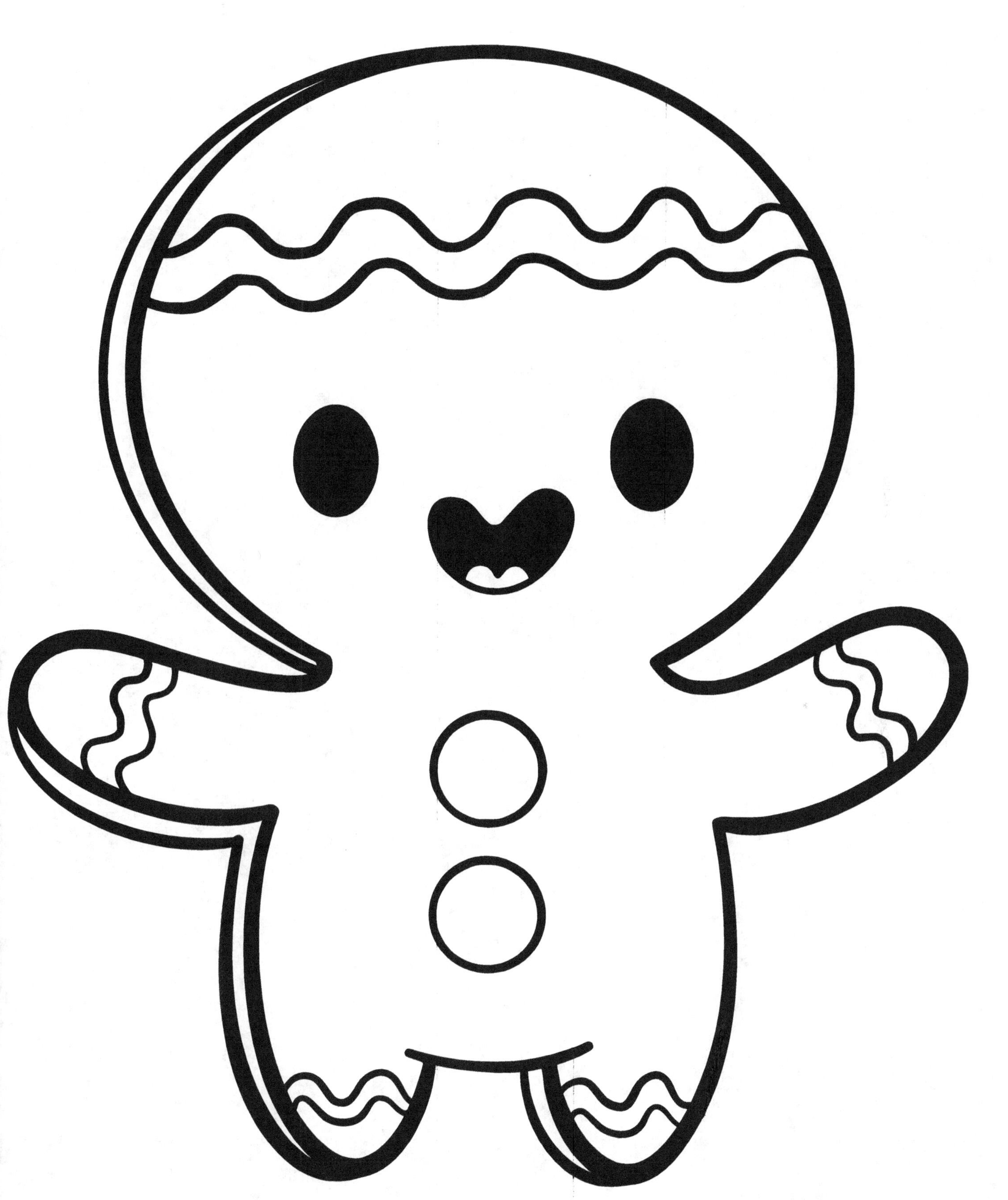

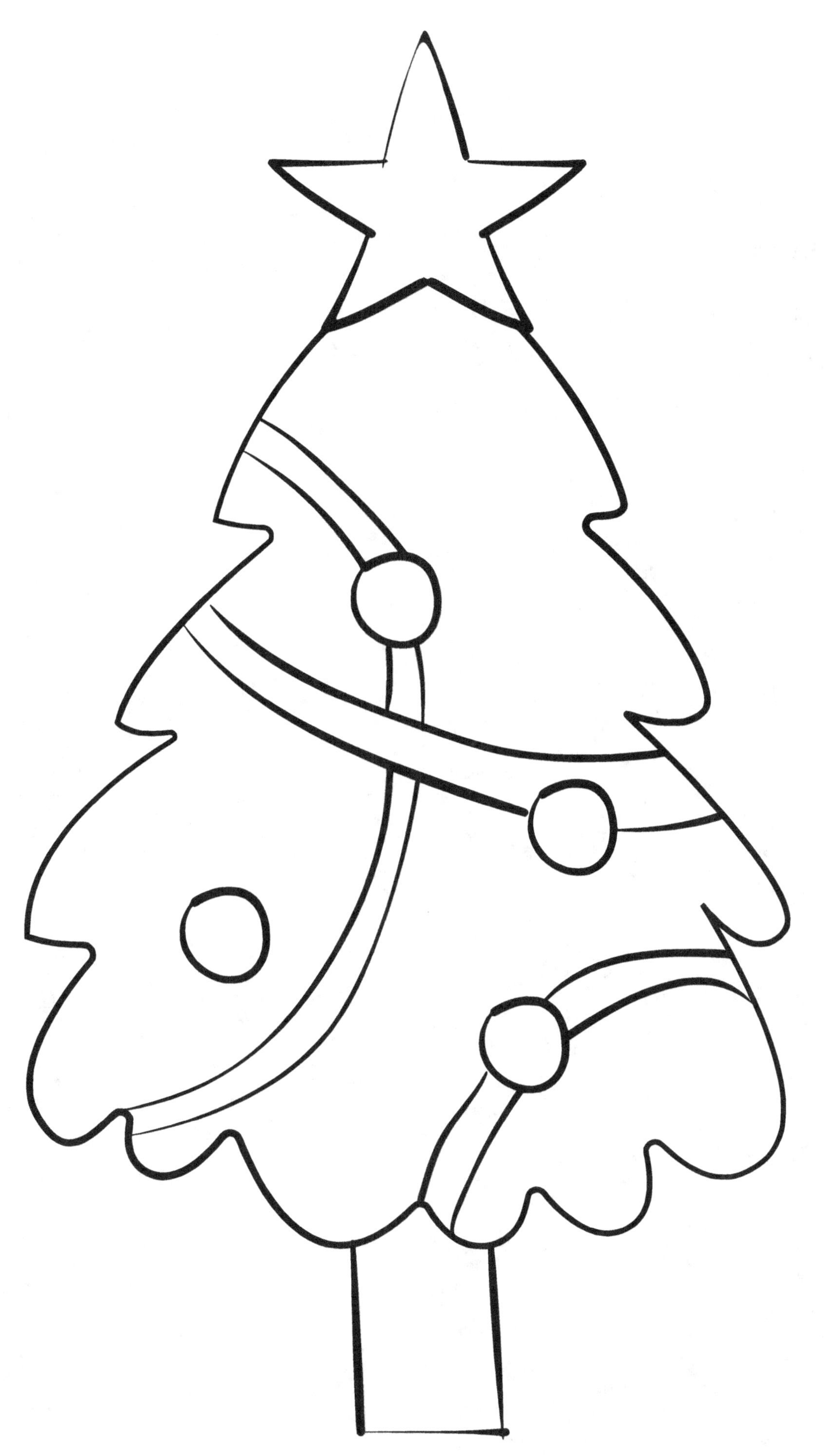

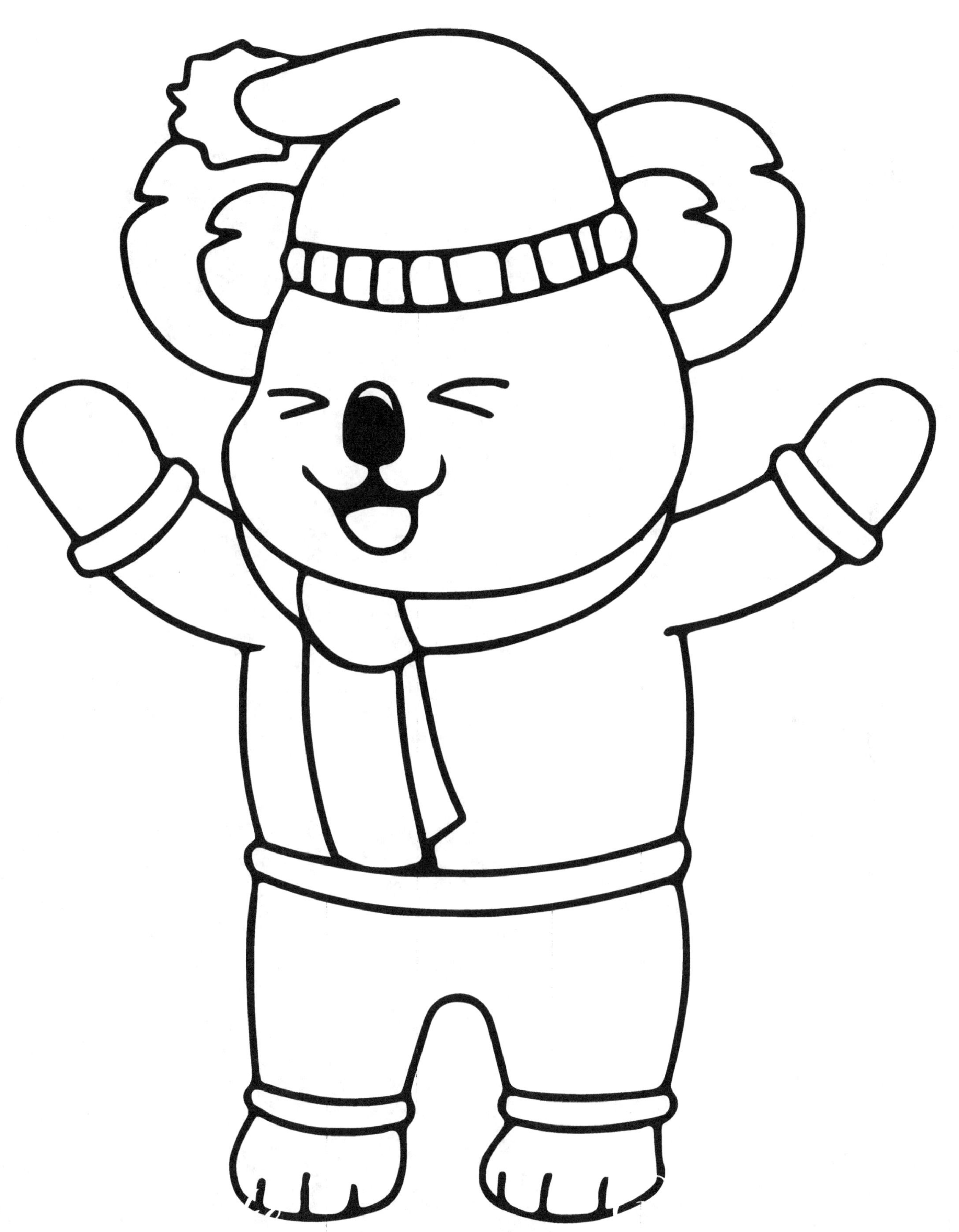

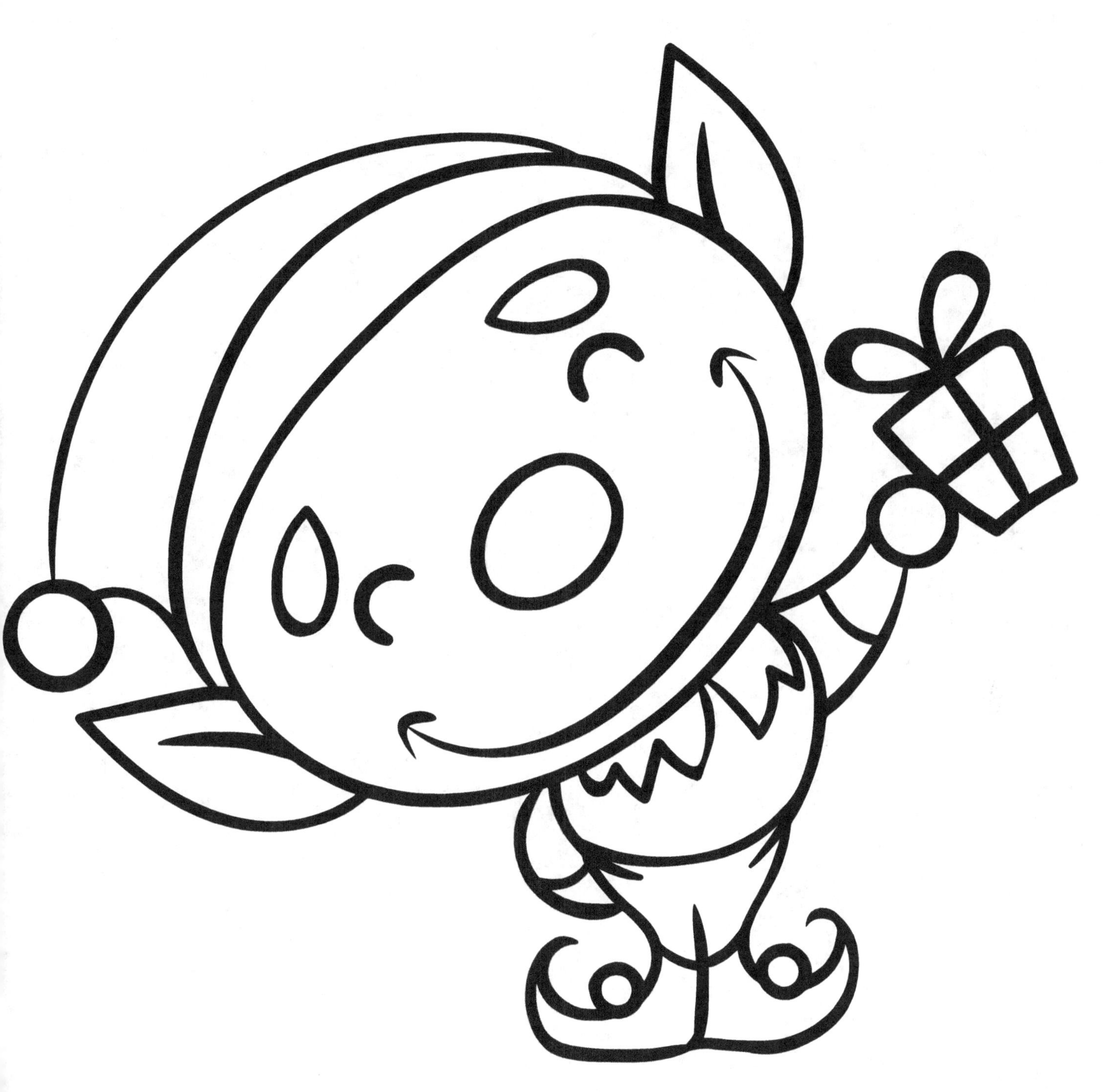

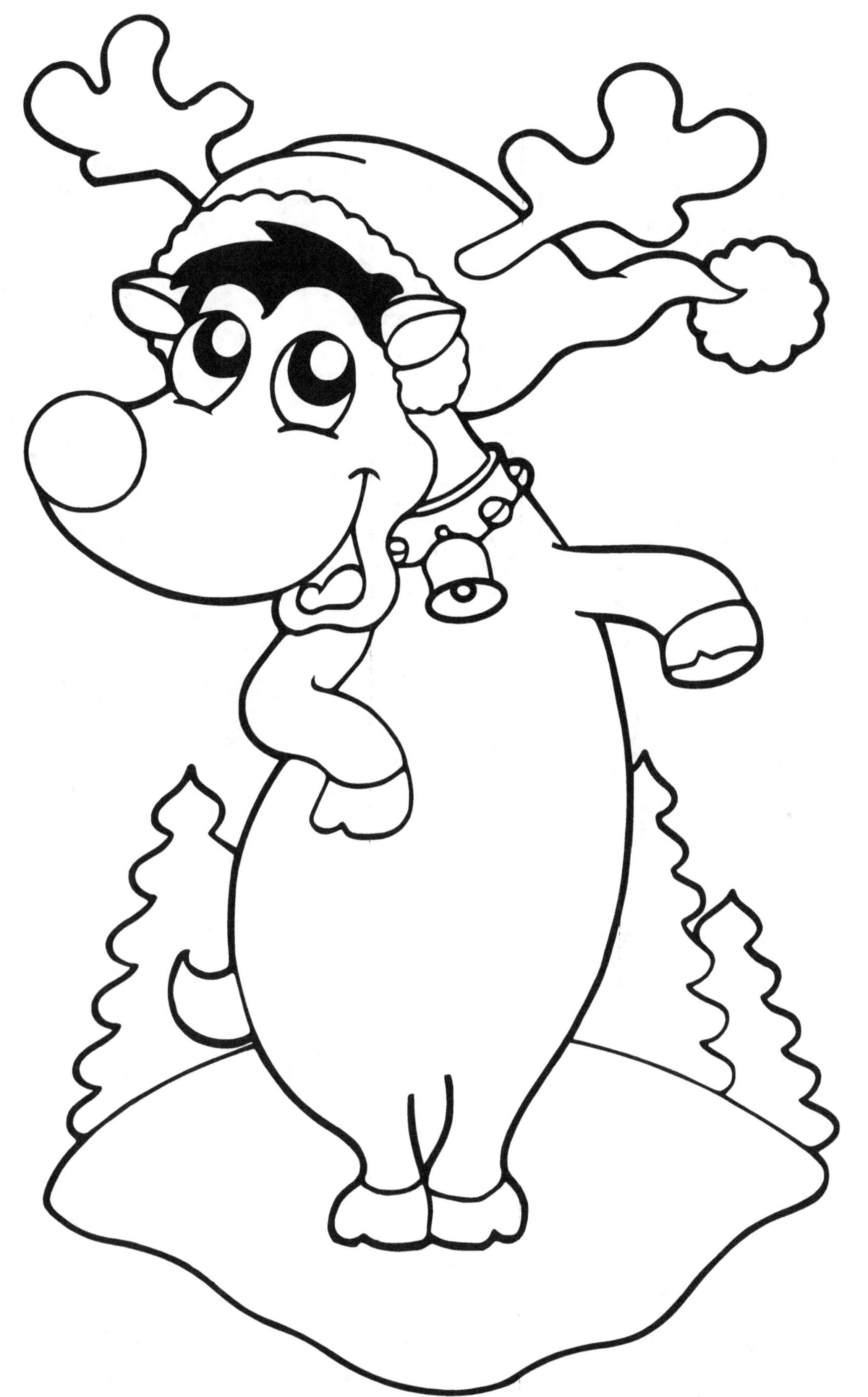

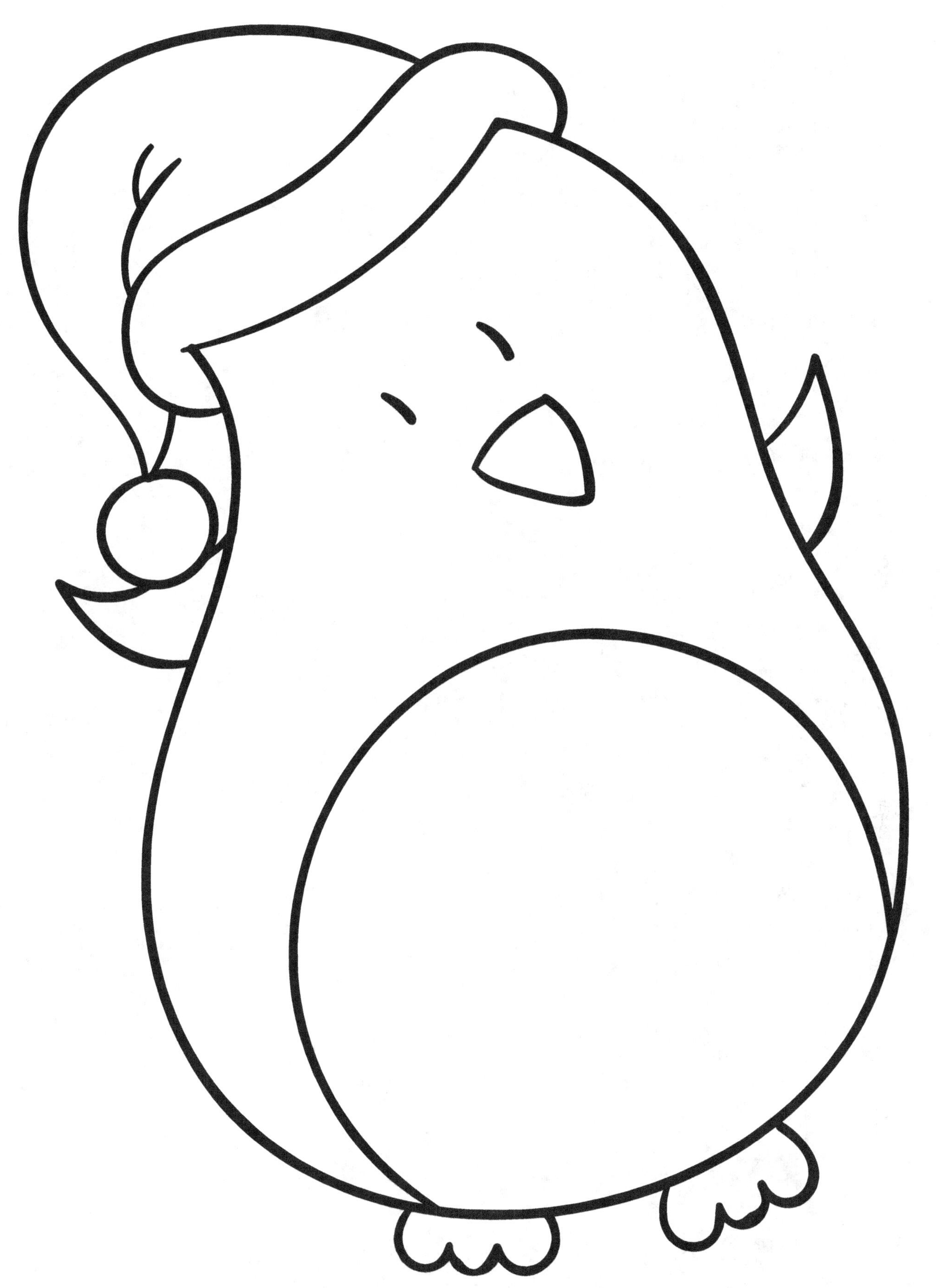

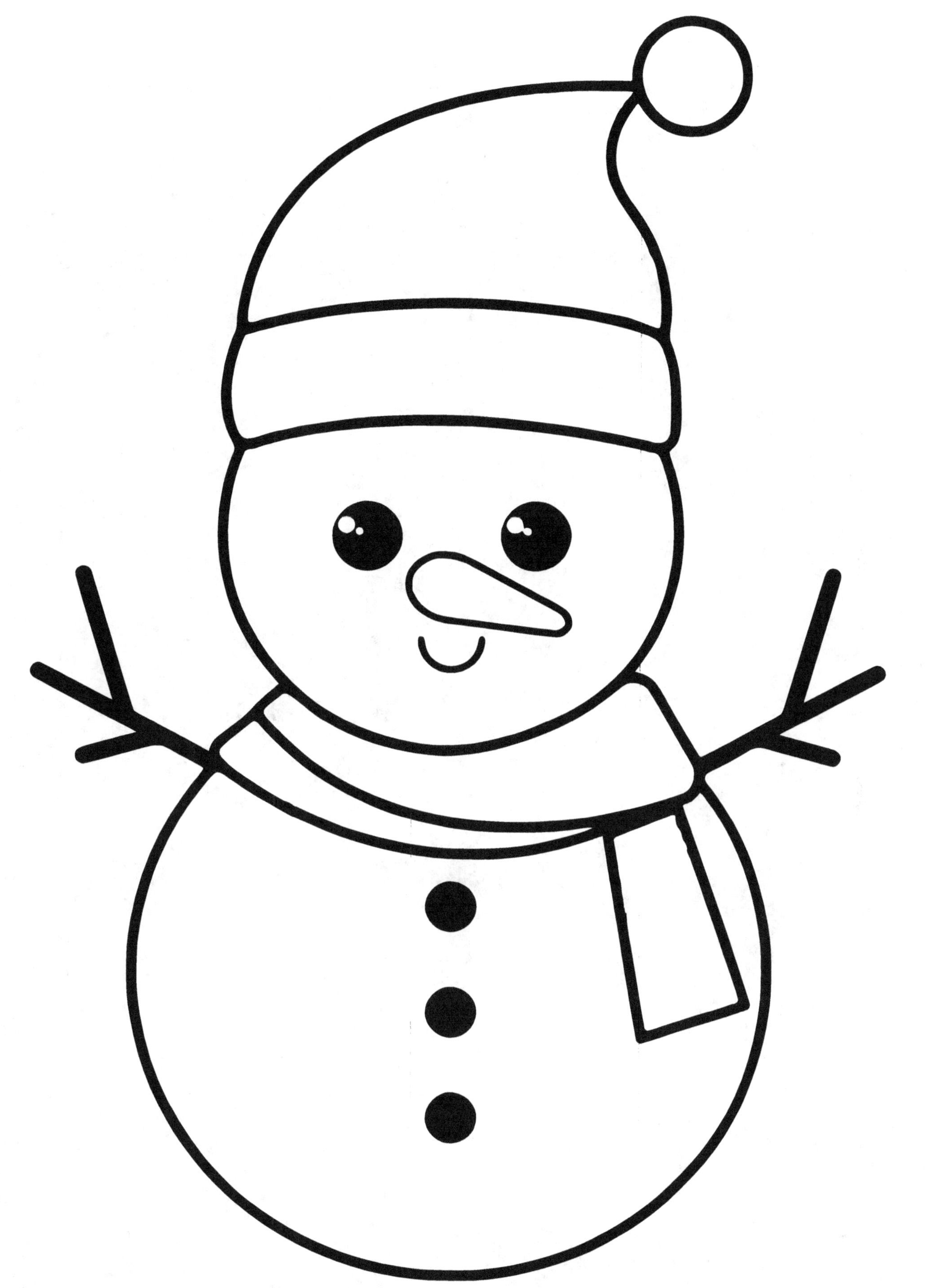

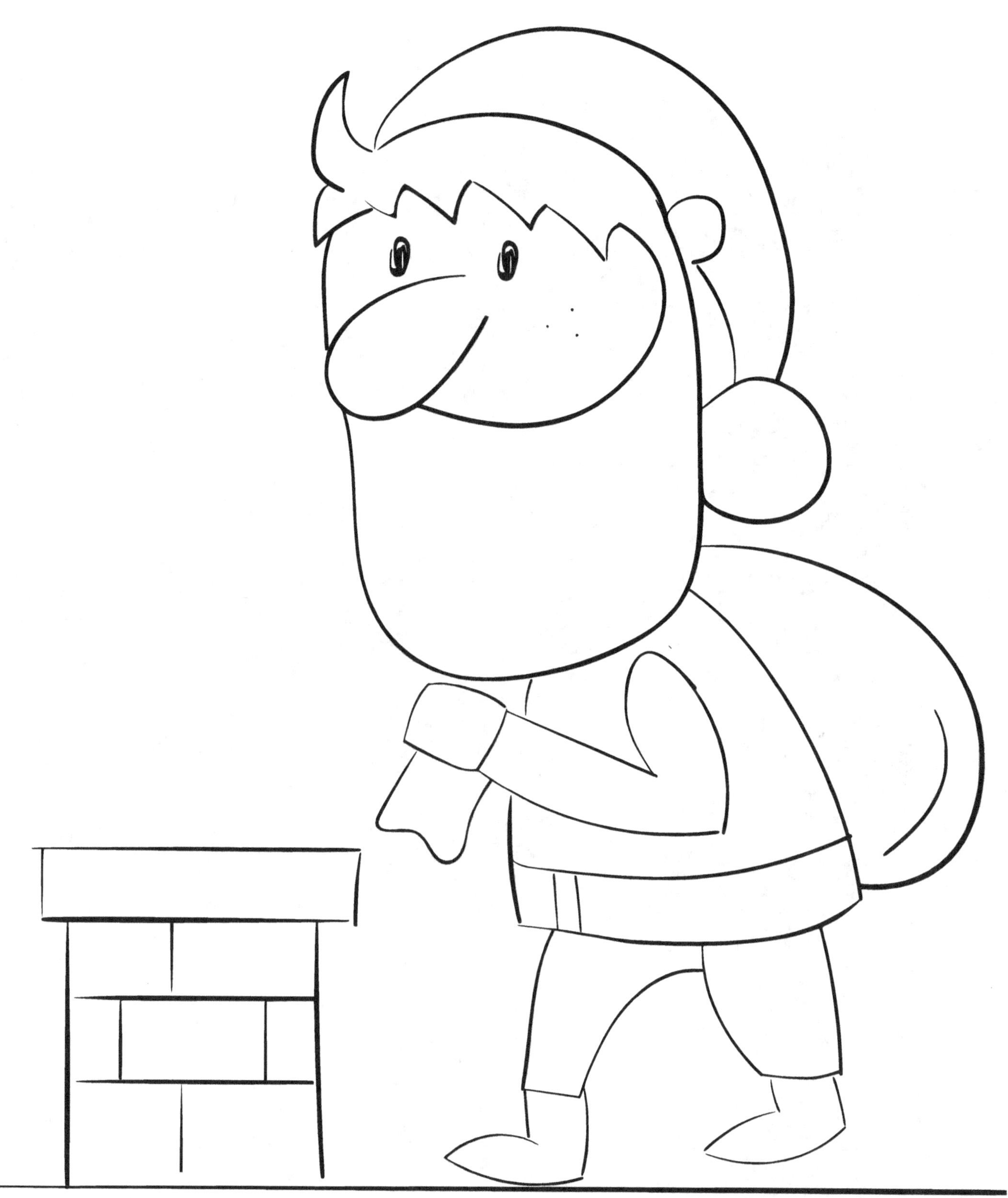

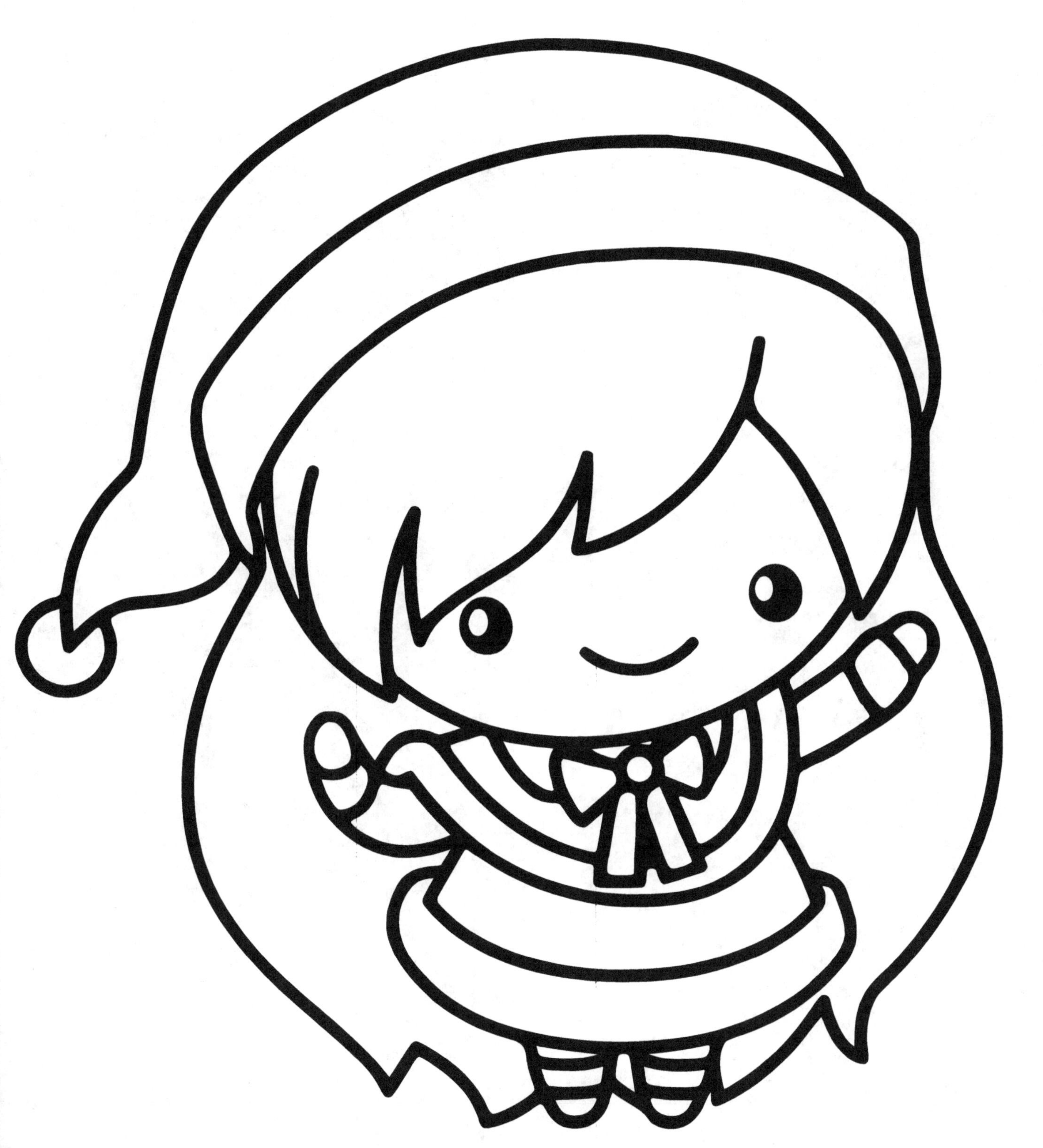

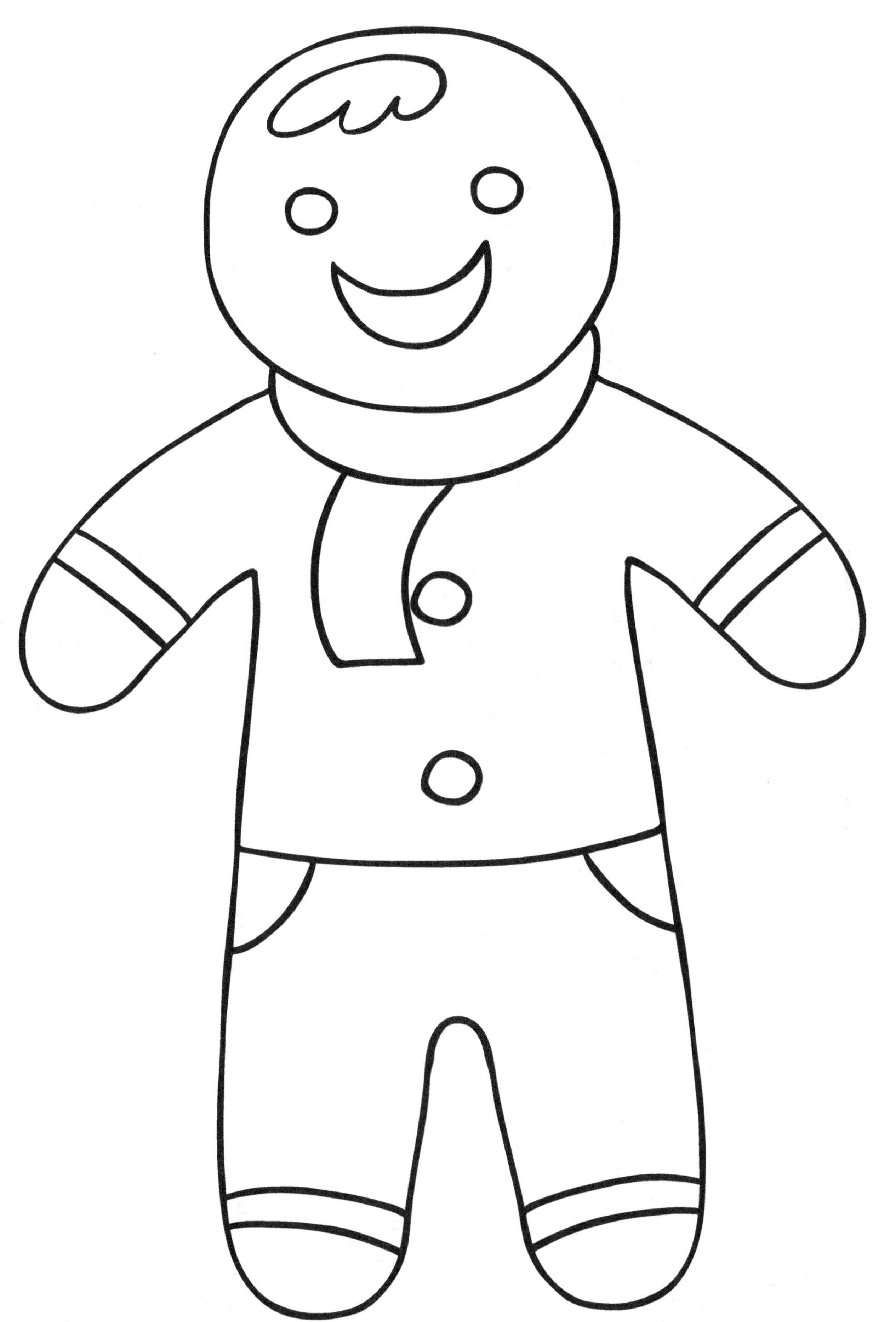

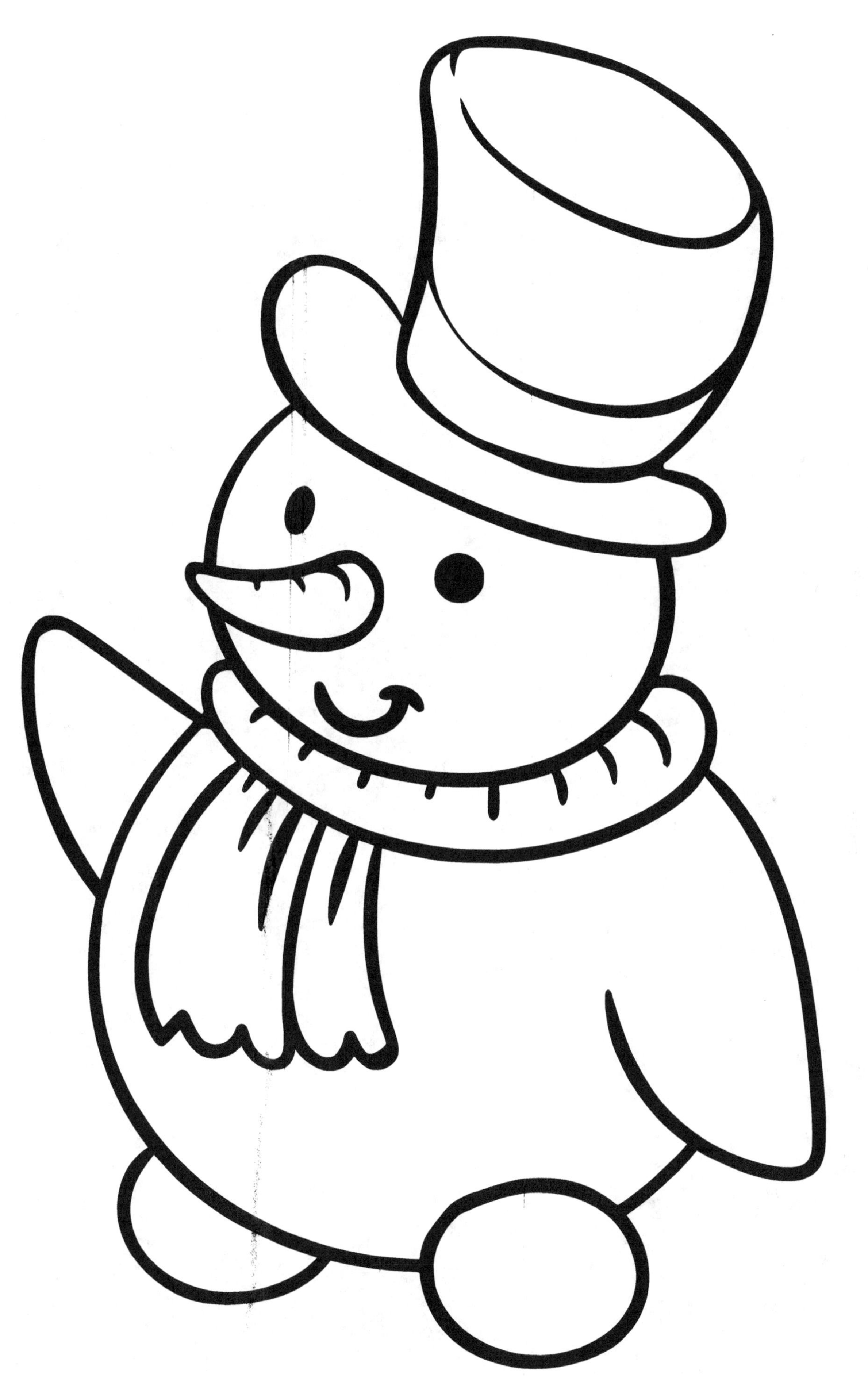